Lerner SPORTS

SPORTS TEAM SMACKDOWN

DALLAS COWBOYS VS. PHILADELPHIA EAGLES

RIVAL RUMBLE

ABBY COLICH

Lerner Publications ◆ Minneapolis

Stats in this book are accurate through the 2025 Super Bowl.

Lerner Publications Company
An imprint of Lerner Publishing Group, Inc.
241 First Avenue North
Minneapolis, MN 55401 USA

For reading levels and more information, look up this title at www.lernerbooks.com.

Main body text set in Aptifer Sans LT Pro. Typeface provided by Linotype AG.

Editor: Matt Doeden

Library of Congress Cataloging-in-Publication Data

Names: Colich, Abby, author.
Title: Dallas Cowboys vs. Philadelphia Eagles : rival rumble / Abigail Colich.
Other titles: Dallas Cowboys versus Philadelphia Eagles
Description: Minneapolis, MN : Lerner Publications, [2026] | Series: Sports team smackdown (Lerner sports) | Includes bibliographical references and index. | Audience: Ages 7–11 | Audience: Grades 4–6 | Summary: "The Dallas Cowboys and Philadelphia Eagles have one of the NFL's oldest rivalries. They have battled in the same division since 1961. Relive the thrilling games and meet the players that make this rivalry special"— Provided by publisher.
Identifiers: LCCN 2024045891 (print) | LCCN 2024045892 (ebook) | ISBN 9798765668634 (library binding) | ISBN 9798765683491 (paperback) | ISBN 9798765681572 (epub)
Subjects: LCSH: Dallas Cowboys (Football team)—History—Juvenile literature. | Philadelphia Eagles (Football team)—History—Juvenile literature. | Sports rivalries—United States—History—Juvenile literature. | Football teams—United States—History—Juvenile literature. | Football players—United States—Juvenile literature.
Classification: LCC GV956.D3 C69 2026 (print) | LCC GV956.D3 (ebook) | DDC 796.332/64097642812—dc23/eng/20250110

LC record available at https://lccn.loc.gov/2024045891
LC ebook record available at https://lccn.loc.gov/2024045892

Manufactured in the United States of America
1-1011973-53831-2/19/2025v

TABLE OF CONTENTS

INTRODUCTION

A ROARING RIVALRY

It was Week 8 of the 2016 National Football League (NFL) season. The Dallas Cowboys trailed their rivals, the Philadelphia Eagles, 23–16 deep in the fourth quarter. Cowboys star quarterback Tony Romo had been injured in the preseason. This left rookie Dak Prescott to run the offense in his place.

Prescott had been a fourth-round pick in the 2016 NFL Draft. He had not expected to play much that season. But with time ticking away, it was up to him to lead his team to a comeback victory.

Eagles running back Darren Sproles carries the ball against the Cowboys in 2016.

Prescott and the rest of the Cowboys made their way down the field. With three minutes to go, Prescott fired a 22-yard pass to wide receiver Dez Bryant for a touchdown. Kicker Dan Bailey made the extra point for the tie. The game was headed to overtime!

Dallas won the coin toss and began overtime with the ball. They started a long drive down the field. With eight minutes left, Prescott passed the ball to rookie running back Ezekiel Elliott. Elliott sprinted all the way down to the Eagles five-yard line. Then Prescott dropped back, quickly looked over the field, and zipped

FAST FACTS

- After many of their players left to fight in World War II (1939–1945), the Eagles and Pittsburgh Steelers combined to form one team for the 1943 NFL season.
- The Cowboys and Eagles have clashed in the playoffs four times.
- In 2002, Brian Dawkins became the first player in NFL history to have a sack, an interception, a fumble recovery, and a receiving touchdown all in the same game.
- The Cowboys have won five Super Bowls in their history.

a pass to tight end Jason Witten. Touchdown! The Cowboys' comeback win was another thrilling game in one of the NFL's most heated rivalries.

Dak Prescott tries to throw a pass after being hit by an Eagles defender.

SMACKDOWN!

CHAPTER 1

Dallas wide receiver Bob Hayes (left) dodges tacklers in a 1965 game against the Eagles. Philadelphia went on to win 35–24.

TWO RICH HISTORIES

The Dallas Cowboys joined the NFL as an expansion team in 1960. They had a winning season, meaning they won more games than they lost, every year from 1966 to 1985. During that time, they played in the Super Bowl five times and won it twice. This success earned them the nickname America's Team. The Cowboys won the Super Bowl again in the 1992, 1993, and 1995 seasons.

The Philadelphia Eagles formed in 1933. It was a rough start. In their first 10 years, they didn't have a single winning season. In 1943, the NFL had a player shortage. Many young men were fighting in World War II. That season, the Eagles and Pittsburgh Steelers combined to form one team. Fans called them the Steagles.

In 1947, the Eagles' bad luck finally started to turn around. Star quarterback Tommy Thompson led them to three straight NFL Championship Games. They won the title in 1948 and 1949.

The Eagles played the Los Angeles Rams in the 1949 NFL Championship Game. Philadelphia beat the Rams 14–0.

Quarterback Donovan McNabb looks for an open receiver.

The Eagles returned to the title game in 1960. They beat the Green Bay Packers 17–13. But this was their last successful season for a long time. They did not make it back to the playoffs for another 18 years. In 1981, they finally made it to the Super Bowl, but lost to the Oakland Raiders.

Quarterback Donovan McNabb led the Eagles in the early 2000s. They lost the 2005 Super Bowl to the New England Patriots. In 2018, they beat the Patriots for Philadelphia's first Super Bowl win. The Eagles won the Super Bowl again in 2025. They crushed the Kansas City Chiefs 40–22.

CHECK IT OUT

Some Cowboys fans believed that the team's blue jerseys were cursed. They had lost every playoff game wearing that color since 1978. Finally, in 2023, they beat the Tampa Bay Buccaneers in a Wild Card game while wearing their blue jerseys.

The Cowboys and Eagles both play in the National Football Conference (NFC) East division. They play each other at least twice each season. They often compete for the top spot in the NFC East rankings, making for a heated rivalry.

The Cowboys and Eagles have met in the playoffs four times. The Cowboys have won three of those games.

Dallas linebacker Sean Lee (right) makes a big hit in a 2016 game against the Eagles.

CHAPTER 2

Dallas wide receiver Drew Pearson scores the winning touchdown in a 1975 playoff game against the Minnesota Vikings.

POWERFUL PLAYS

Fans have seen many exciting moments from both the Cowboys and Eagles. Here are just a few of the most memorable.

With 32 seconds left in a 1975 playoff game, the Cowboys trailed the Minnesota Vikings 14–10. Dallas quarterback Roger Staubach threw a long, desperate pass. Wide receiver Drew Pearson caught it and stepped into the end zone for a touchdown. The Cowboys won 17–14.

On January 17, 1993, a young Cowboys team was the underdog against the San Francisco 49ers in the NFC Championship Game. It was tied at halftime. Then the Cowboys took control. They went on to win the game 30–20. Two weeks later, they won the Super Bowl.

Wide receiver CeeDee Lamb caught a 92-yard touchdown pass from Dak Prescott against the Detroit Lions on December 30, 2023. It was the longest pass play for the Cowboys since 1966. The team went on to win 20–19.

CeeDee Lamb catches a pass against the Lions in 2023.

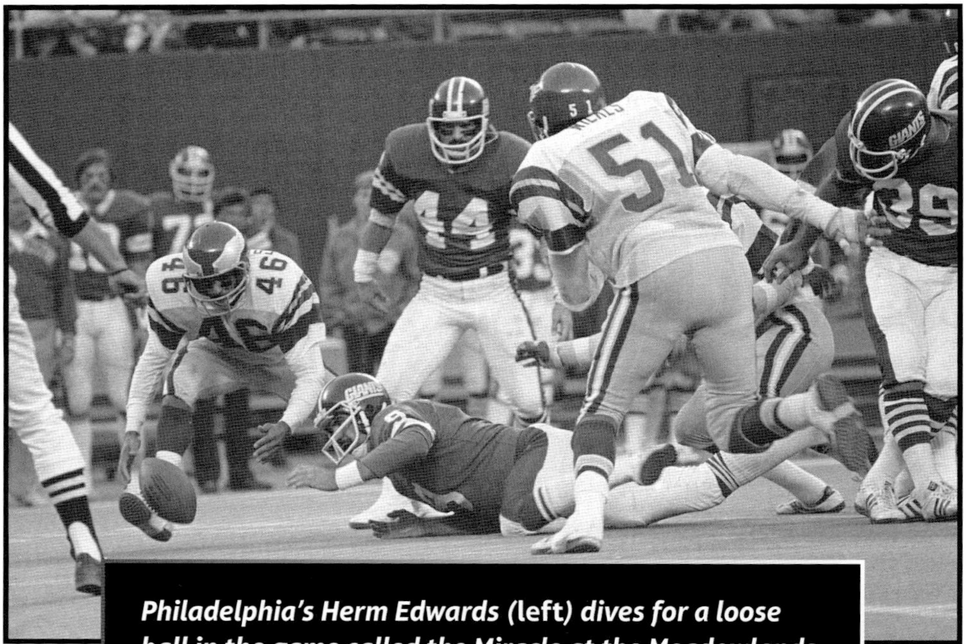

Philadelphia's Herm Edwards (left) dives for a loose ball in the game called the Miracle at the Meadowlands.

Two of the Eagles' greatest moments came against the New York Giants. On November 19, 1978, the Giants led 17–12 with 30 seconds to go. Cornerback Herm Edwards recovered a fumble and ran 26 yards for a touchdown—and the win. The game became known as the Miracle at the Meadowlands after the sports complex where the Giants play.

On December 19, 2010, the Eagles trailed the Giants 31–10 with eight minutes left. The Eagles scored three quick touchdowns. Then on the last play, wide receiver DeSean Jackson returned a punt for a final game-winning touchdown. The win became known as the Miracle at the Meadowlands Two.

During the 2018 Super Bowl, the Eagles ended the first half with a trick play known as the Philly Special. Tight end Trey Burton passed the ball to quarterback Nick Foles for a touchdown. The play helped the Eagles beat the Patriots 41–33.

Trey Burton (right) prepares to catch the ball before throwing a touchdown pass in the Super Bowl.

Eagles defenders chase Cowboys running back Calvin Hill in this 1969 game.

The Cowboys and Eagles rivalry has had its own tense moments. Even their first meeting in 1960 had plenty of excitement. A 75-yard pass from quarterback Eddie LeBaron to wide receiver Frank Clarke put the Cowboys within one point of the Eagles in the third quarter. But the Eagles pulled off the win 27–25.

CHECK IT OUT

Fans call the Eagles versus Cowboys game on September 3, 2000, the Pickle Juice Game. The temperature in Dallas was 109°F (43°C). Eagles players drank pickle juice during the game to help stop muscle cramps. It worked. The Eagles won 41–14.

On January 9, 2010, the Cowboys played the Eagles in a playoff game. Running back Felix Jones scored on a 73-yard touchdown run in the third quarter. The Eagles couldn't keep up. The Cowboys won 34–14.

With less than two minutes to play on December 9, 2018, Eagles quarterback Carson Wentz passed to Darren Sproles for a touchdown to force overtime. Then Cowboys quarterback Dak Prescott took over. He threw a short 15-yard touchdown pass to Amari Cooper to give Dallas the win 29–23.

Dallas running back Felix Jones breaks free for a 73-yard touchdown run in this 2010 playoff game.

CHAPTER 3

Defensive tackle Bob "Mr. Cowboy" Lilly (left) is a Dallas football legend.

GREATEST PLAYERS

Some of the NFL's greatest have played for the Cowboys. Bob Lilly was a defensive tackle for the team from 1961 to 1974. Nicknamed Mr. Cowboy, he led the team in sacks for three seasons. Lilly's dominance on the field was a major reason the Miami Dolphins scored only three points in the 1972 Super Bowl. That's the lowest Super Bowl score ever.

Quarterback Roger Staubach played for the Cowboys from 1969 to 1979. During his career, no quarterback outplayed him. He helped the Cowboys stage 13 fourth quarter comebacks, giving him the nickname Captain Comeback.

Running back Tony Dorsett played for the Cowboys from 1977 to 1987. In that time, he scored 72 touchdowns. He had more than 1,000 rushing yards in eight of those seasons. In 1983, he ran 99 yards to score a touchdown against the Vikings. Dorsett and Derrick Henry are the only players in NFL history with 99-yard touchdown runs.

Tony Dorsett (left) was one of the league's best running backs in the 1980s.

Three of the Cowboys' greatest players ever, quarterback Troy Aikman, running back Emmitt Smith, and wide receiver Michael Irvin, are known as the Triplets. They led a powerful Dallas offense in the early 1990s. Together they helped the team win three Super Bowls.

The Cowboys drafted defensive end Micah Parsons in the 2021 NFL Draft. That year, he had the fourth most sacks by a rookie in the history of the NFL. For this, he was named Defensive Rookie of the Year.

Linebacker Micah Parsons (left) rushes the quarterback in this 2024 game against the Houston Texans.

Chuck Bednarik was a hard-hitting player who starred at both linebacker and center for the Eagles.

The Eagles have also had many amazing stars. Speedy running back Steve Van Buren played from 1944 to 1951. In 1945 he led the NFL in rushing, scoring, and average kickoff return yards.

Chuck Bednarik played as a linebacker and center for the Eagles from 1949 to 1962. He helped the Eagles win NFL Championships in 1949 and 1960 and only missed three games during his career.

Wide receiver Harold Carmichael (right) holds many Eagles records.

Harold Carmichael was a wide receiver for the Eagles from 1971 to 1983. He led the team to their first Super Bowl in 1981. He played 180 games for the Eagles and holds team records for touchdowns, pass catches, and receiving yards.

CHECK IT OUT

The Cowboys dominated the rivalry with the Eagles in the early 1990s. But in 1991, the Eagles had an amazing game. They sacked Troy Aikman 11 times in one game! Philadelphia won 24–0.

Defensive end Reggie White played for the Eagles from 1985 to 1992. He still holds the team record for most sacks with 124. Many fans consider White to be the best defender in NFL history.

Brian Dawkins was a safety for the Eagles from 1996 to 2008. In 2002, he became the first NFL player to have a sack, interception, fumble recovery, and touchdown catch all in the same game.

Brian Dawkins was one of the stars of the Eagles defense in the early 2000s.

Quarterback Donovan McNabb was Philadelphia's quarterback from 1999 to 2009. He holds Eagles records for most pass attempts, passes completed, passing yards, and touchdown passes.

The Eagles drafted quarterback Jalen Hurts in 2020. In 2023, he led the team to the Super Bowl. The Eagles lost to the Kansas City Chiefs. In 2025, Hurts and the Eagles reached the Super Bowl again. He won the Super Bowl MVP award after throwing two touchdown passes and leading his team to victory over the Chiefs.

Quarterback Jalen Hurts hands the ball to running back Saquon Barkley in this 2024 game against the Rams.

CHAPTER 4

Eagles wide receiver Johnny Wilson hauls in a touchdown pass in this 2024 win over the Cowboys.

CHOOSE YOUR CHAMPION

Do you ever compare your favorite team to their top rival? Looking at your team against their rivals keeps sports fun and interesting. Let's compare the Cowboys and the Eagles. Which team comes out on top?

The Cowboys have won more than 57 percent of all their games since joining the league. The Eagles have won a little less than half of their games. The Cowboys have a better playoff record at 36–31. The Eagles' playoff record is 25–26. The Cowboys have won five Super Bowls. The Eagles have won two. And the Cowboys lead the series rivalry 74–56.

Although the Eagles are the older team, the Cowboys have had more success in a shorter time. They are the winner in this smackdown. Do you agree? Who do you choose?

Eagles and Cowboys players reach for the ball during a 2024 game.

Running back Rico Dowdle carries the ball as Eagles defenders try to tackle him in 2024.

SMACKDOWN TIMELINE

DALLAS COWBOYS

1960 The Cowboys join the NFL as an expansion team.

1972 The Cowboys win their first Super Bowl.

1978 The Cowboys win their second Super Bowl.

1993 The Cowboys win their third Super Bowl.

1994 The Cowboys win their fourth Super Bowl.

1996 The Cowboys win their fifth Super Bowl.

2002 Cowboys running back Emmitt Smith becomes the NFL's career rushing leader.

2009 The Cowboys win their first playoff game in thirteen years.

2024 The Cowboys have their first losing record in four seasons and fire head coach Mike McCarthy.

PHILADELPHIA EAGLES

1933 The Eagles begin their first season in the NFL.

1948 The Eagles win their first NFL Championship.

1949 The Eagles win their second NFL Championship.

1960 The Eagles win their third NFL Championship.

1981 The Eagles win a playoff game for the first time since 1960.

2005 The Eagles reach the Super Bowl for the first time, but lose to the New England Patriots.

2018 The Eagles beat the Patriots to win their first Super Bowl.

2023 The Eagles lose to the Kansas City Chiefs in the Super Bowl.

2025 The Eagles beat the Chiefs in the Super Bowl.

GLOSSARY

complex: a group of closely related buildings

cornerback: a defensive player who usually covers the opponents' wide receivers

division: a group of teams that directly compete against one another

drive: a series of football plays

expansion team: a new team added to an existing league

MVP: Most Valuable Player

NFL Championship: the NFL's championship game before the Super Bowl

rivalry: being in direct competition with an athlete or team

rookie: a first-year player

sack: when the quarterback is tackled for a loss of yards

underdog: a team expected by most to lose a game

wild card: a team that makes the playoffs despite not winning its division

LEARN MORE

Anderson, Josh. *Inside the Philadelphia Eagles*. Minneapolis: Lerner Publications, 2024.

Britannica Kids: Dallas Cowboys
https://kids.britannica.com/students/article/Dallas-Cowboys/571006

Britannica Kids: Philadelphia Eagles
https://kids.britannica.com/students/article/Philadelphia-Eagles/571021

Doeden, Matt. *Meet Jalen Hurts*. Minneapolis: Lerner Publications, 2024.

Goodman, Michael. *Dallas Cowboys*. Mankato, MN: Creative Education/Creative Paperbacks, 2023.

Pro Football Hall of Fame: Dallas Cowboys Facts
https://www.profootballhof.com/teams/dallas-cowboys/team-facts/

INDEX

PHOTO ACKNOWLEDGMENTS

Image credits: Ray Carlin/Icon Sportswire/Getty Images, p. 4; Steve Nurenberg/Icon Sportswire/Getty Images, p. 6; AP Photo/Terrance Williams, p. 7 (top); AP Photo/Brynn Anderson, p. 7 (bottom); Rolls Press/Popperfoto/Getty Images, p. 8; Vic Stein/Getty Images, p. 9; George Gojkovich/Getty Images, p. 10; Ray Carlin/Icon Sportswire/Getty Images, p. 11; AP Photo, pp. 12, 19, 21; AP Photo/Jeff Nguyen/Detroit Lions, p. 13; AP Photo/G. Paul Burnett, p. 14; Simon Bruty/*Sports Illustrated*/Getty Images, p. 15; Focus on Sport/Getty Images, p. 16; AP Photo/G. Newman Lowrance, p. 17; AP Photo/Tony Tomsic, p. 18; AP Photo/Matt Patterson, p. 20; AP Photo/Gene Puskar, p. 22; AP Photo/Icon Sportswire, p. 23; AP Photo/Mark J. Terrill, p. 24; AP Photo/Richard W. Rodriguez, pp. 25, 26; Sam Hodde/Getty Images, p. 27. Design elements: Trisno Wardana/Shutterstock; Ihor Biliavskyi/Shutterstock; Joko Ribowo/Shutterstock.

Cover: AP Photo/Kevin Terrell; AP Photo/Matt Slocum.